G000294606

TRAVEL JOURNAL
Photographs by Chris Caldicott

F

FRANCES LINCOLN LIMITED

PUBLISHERS

Frances Lincoln Limited
4 Torriano Mews
Torriano Avenue
London NW5 2RZ
www.franceslincoln.com

Travel Journal
Copyright © Frances Lincoln Limited 2010
All photographs copyright © Chris Caldicott
except Petra and Palmyra copyright © Martin and Lisa Oestreicher

All rights reserved. No part of this publication may be reproduced, stored
in a retrieval system or transmitted, in any form, or by any means,
electronic, mechanical, photocopying, recording or otherwise, without
either prior permission in writing from the publishers or a licence
permitting restricted copying. In the United Kingdom such licences are
issued by the Copyright Licensing Agency, Saffron House,
6–10 Kirby Street, London EC1N 8TS.

A catalogue record for this book is available
from the British Library

Designed by Becky Clarke

ISBN 978-0-7112-3124-5

Printed in Hong Kong
First Frances Lincoln edition 2010

USING THIS BOOK

Every journey needs some organization and, with a little planning before you set out, valuable time can be saved when you are *en route*. This journal is the ideal place to list your travel arrangements – train times, flight numbers and other essential information – together with recommendations for places to visit, stay or eat, gathered from friends or guidebooks. Using this book, your time can be as carefully planned or as spontaneous as you wish.

The 'Journal' section is the place to write about your experiences or to make sketches of the places you explore: the sights and sounds, the unfolding landscapes, the people you meet and the discoveries you make.

At the back of the book, you will find conversion tables and useful information about countries you may visit or pass through, as well as space to keep track of budgets and make a note of useful addresses.

PERSONAL INFORMATION

NAME _____

ADDRESS _____

_____

_____

TELEPHONE _____

MOBILE _____

FAX _____

E-MAIL ADDRESS _____

PASSPORT NO. _____

DRIVING LICENCE NO. _____

MEDICAL INFORMATION _____

_____

_____

IN CASE OF EMERGENCY, PLEASE CONTACT

NAME _____

ADDRESS _____

_____

_____

TELEPHONE _____

MOBILE _____

Rajsamand, India

TRAVEL DETAILS

PLANNING AND PACKING

Polonnaruwa, Sri Lanka

PLANNING AND PACKING

ITINERARIES

DATES	PLACE
_____ TO _____	_____
_____ TO _____	_____
_____ TO _____	_____
_____ TO _____	_____
_____ TO _____	_____
_____ TO _____	_____
_____ TO _____	_____
_____ TO _____	_____
_____ TO _____	_____
_____ TO _____	_____
_____ TO _____	_____
_____ TO _____	_____
_____ TO _____	_____
_____ TO _____	_____
_____ TO _____	_____
_____ TO _____	_____
_____ TO _____	_____
_____ TO _____	_____
_____ TO _____	_____
_____ TO _____	_____

ITINERARIES

_____ TO _____   _____

_____ TO _____   _____

_____ TO _____   _____

_____ TO _____   _____

_____ TO _____   _____

_____ TO _____   _____

_____ TO _____   _____

_____ TO _____   _____

_____ TO _____   _____

_____ TO _____   _____

_____ TO _____   _____

_____ TO _____   _____

_____ TO _____   _____

_____ TO _____   _____

_____ TO _____   _____

_____ TO _____   _____

_____ TO _____   _____

_____ TO _____   _____

_____ TO _____   _____

_____ TO _____   _____

_____ TO _____   _____

_____ TO _____   _____

_____ TO _____   _____

_____ TO _____   _____

_____ TO _____   _____

Nevis, Caribbean

ITINERARIES

DATES	PLACE

_____ TO _____

_____ TO _____

_____ TO _____

_____ TO _____

_____ TO _____

_____ TO _____

_____ TO _____

_____ TO _____

_____ TO _____

_____ TO _____

_____ TO _____

_____ TO _____

_____ TO _____

_____ TO _____

_____ TO _____

_____ TO _____

_____ TO _____

_____ TO _____

_____ TO _____

_____ TO _____

_____ TO _____

_____ TO _____

_____ TO _____

_____ TO _____

_____ TO _____

_____ TO _____

_____ TO _____

ITINERARIES

DATES		PLACE
————————	TO ————————	—————————————————————
————————	TO ————————	—————————————————————
————————	TO ————————	—————————————————————
————————	TO ————————	—————————————————————
————————	TO ————————	—————————————————————
————————	TO ————————	—————————————————————
————————	TO ————————	—————————————————————
————————	TO ————————	—————————————————————
————————	TO ————————	—————————————————————
————————	TO ————————	—————————————————————
————————	TO ————————	—————————————————————
————————	TO ————————	—————————————————————
————————	TO ————————	—————————————————————
————————	TO ————————	—————————————————————
————————	TO ————————	—————————————————————
————————	TO ————————	—————————————————————
————————	TO ————————	—————————————————————
————————	TO ————————	—————————————————————
————————	TO ————————	—————————————————————
————————	TO ————————	—————————————————————
————————	TO ————————	—————————————————————
————————	TO ————————	—————————————————————
————————	TO ————————	—————————————————————
————————	TO ————————	—————————————————————
————————	TO ————————	—————————————————————
————————	TO ————————	—————————————————————
————————	TO ————————	—————————————————————
————————	TO ————————	—————————————————————

Rome, Italy

ITINERARIES

DATES	PLACE

_____ TO _____

_____ TO _____

_____ TO _____

_____ TO _____

_____ TO _____

_____ TO _____

_____ TO _____

_____ TO _____

_____ TO _____

_____ TO _____

_____ TO _____

_____ TO _____

_____ TO _____

_____ TO _____

_____ TO _____

_____ TO _____

_____ TO _____

_____ TO _____

_____ TO _____

_____ TO _____

_____ TO _____

_____ TO _____

_____ TO _____

_____ TO _____

_____ TO _____

_____ TO _____

_____ TO _____

ITINERARIES

ATES   PLACE

_____ TO _____   _____
_____ TO _____   _____
_____ TO _____   _____
_____ TO _____   _____
_____ TO _____   _____
_____ TO _____   _____
_____ TO _____   _____
_____ TO _____   _____
_____ TO _____   _____
_____ TO _____   _____
_____ TO _____   _____
_____ TO _____   _____
_____ TO _____   _____
_____ TO _____   _____
_____ TO _____   _____
_____ TO _____   _____
_____ TO _____   _____
_____ TO _____   _____
_____ TO _____   _____

PLACES TO VISIT

DATE	DETAILS

DATE   DETAILS

PLACES TO VISIT

DATE	DETAILS

PLACES TO VISIT

DETAILS

San Francisco, USA

PLACES TO VISIT

DATE	DETAILS

PLACES TO VISIT

DATE   DETAILS

PLACES TO STAY

NAME	ADDRESS AND TELEPHONE NUMBER

Corniglia, Italy

PLACES TO STAY

NAME	ADDRESS AND TELEPHONE NUMBER	NOTES

PLACES TO STAY

NAME	ADDRESS AND TELEPHONE NUMBER	NOTES

PLACES TO STAY

NAME	ADDRESS AND TELEPHONE NUMBER	NOTES

PLACES TO STAY

NAME	ADDRESS AND TELEPHONE NUMBER	NOTES

PLACES TO STAY

NAME   ADDRESS AND TELEPHONE NUMBER

Phuket, Thailand

PLACES TO EAT

NAME	ADDRESS AND TELEPHONE NUMBER	NOTES

NAME	ADDRESS AND TELEPHONE NUMBER	NOTES

Marrakesh, Morocco

PLACES TO EAT

NAME	ADDRESS AND TELEPHONE NUMBER

PLACES TO EAT

NAME	ADDRESS AND TELEPHONE NUMBER	NOTES

PLACES TO EAT

NAME	ADDRESS AND TELEPHONE NUMBER	NOTES

PLACES TO EAT

NAME	ADDRESS AND TELEPHONE NUMBER	NOTES

Huang Shan, China

JOURNAL

Previous pages: Venice, Italy

Hunza Valley, Pakistan

JOURNAL

JOURNAL

Venice, Italy

JOURNAL

JOURNAL

JOURNAL

JOURNAL

Dubai, UAE

JOURNAL

JOURNAL

Lock Fyne, Scotland

JOURNAL

JOURNAL

JOURNAL

JOURNAL

Mahé, Seychelles

JOURNAL

JOURNAL

Trincomalee, Sri Lanka

JOURNAL

JOURNAL

JOURNAL

Phnom Penh, Cambodia

JOURNAL

JOURNAL

Ghorka region, Nepal

JOURNAL

JOURNAL

JOURNAL

JOURNAL

New York, USA

JOURNAL

JOURNAL

Barcelona, Spain

JOURNAL

JOURNAL

JOURNAL

Jaipur, India

JOURNAL

JOURNAL

Petra, Jordan

BUDGETS

DATE	DETAILS	AMOUNT	

BUDGETS

DATE	DETAILS	AMOUNT	

BUDGETS

DATE	DETAILS	AMOUNT	

BUDGETS

DATE	DETAILS	AMOUNT	

BUDGETS

DATE	DETAILS	AMOUNT	

BUDGETS

DATE	DETAILS	AMOUNT	

INTERNATIONAL INFORMATION

COUNTRY	DIALLING CODE	HOURS DIFF. FROM GMT	COUNTRY	DIALLING CODE	HOURS DIFF. FROM GMT
Afghanistan	93	+4½	Chad	235	+1
Albania	355	+1	Chile	56	-4
Algeria	213	+1	China	86	+8
Andorra	376	+1	Christmas Island	61	+7
Angola	244	+1	Colombia	57	-5
Anguilla	1264	-4	Comoros	269	+3
Antigua and Barbuda	1268	-4	Congo	242	+1
Argentina	54	-3	Cook Islands	682	-10
Armenia	374	+4	Costa Rica	506	-6
Aruba	297	-4	Côte d'Ivoire	225	0
Ascension Island	247	0	Croatia	385	+1
Australia	61	+8/+10	Cuba	53	-5
Austria	43	+1	Cyprus	357	+2
Azerbaijan	994	+5	Czech Republic	420	+1
Bahamas	1242	-5	DR Congo	243	+2
Bahrain	973	+3	Denmark	45	+1
Bangladesh	880	+6	Diego Garcia	246	+5
Barbados	1246	-4	Djibouti	253	+3
Belarus	375	+2	Dominica	1767	-4
Belgium	32	+1	Dominican Republic	1809	-4
Belize	501	-6	Ecuador	593	-5
Benin	229	+1	Egypt	20	+2
Bermuda	1441	-4	El Salvador	503	-6
Bhutan	975	+6	Equatorial Guinea	240	+1
Bolivia	591	-4	Eritrea	291	+3
Bosnia-Herzegovina	387	+1	Estonia	372	+2
Botswana	267	+2	Ethiopia	251	+3
Brazil	55	-3	Falkland Islands	500	-4
Brunei	673	+8	Faroe Islands	298	0
Bulgaria	359	+2	Fiji	679	+12
Burkina Faso	226	0	Finland	358	+2
Burundi	257	+2	France	33	+1
Cambodia	855	+7	French Guiana	594	-3
Cameroon	237	+1	French Polynesia	689	-10
Canada	1	-3½/-8	Gabon	241	+1
Cape Verde	238	-1	Gambia	220	0
Cayman Islands	1345	-5	Georgia	995	+4
Central African Republic	236	+1	Germany	49	+1

COUNTRY	DIALLING CODE	HOURS DIFF. FROM GMT	COUNTRY	DIALLING CODE	HOURS DIFF. FROM GMT
Ghana	233	0	Lithuania	370	+2
Gibraltar	350	+1	Luxembourg	352	+1
Greece	30	+2	Macao	853	+8
Greenland	299	-4	Macedonia	389	+1
Grenada	1473	-4	Madagascar	261	+3
Guadeloupe	590	-4	Malawi	265	+2
Guam	1671	+10	Malaysia	60	+8
Guatemala	502	-6	Maldives	960	+5
Guinea	224	0	Mali	223	0
Guinea-Bissau	245	0	Malta	356	+1
Guyana	592	-4	Marshall Islands	692	+12
Haiti	509	-5	Martinique	596	-4
Honduras	504	-6	Mauritania	222	0
Hong Kong	852	+8	Mauritius	230	+4
Hungary	36	+1	Mayotte	269	+3
Iceland	354	0	Mexico	52	-5/-7
India	91	+5½	Micronesia	691	+10/+11
Indonesia	62	+7/+9	Moldova	373	+2
Iran	98	+3½	Monaco	377	+1
Iraq	964	+3	Mongolia	976	+8
Ireland	353	0	Montserrat	1664	-4
Israel	972	+2	Morocco	212	0
Italy	39	+1	Mozambique	258	+2
Jamaica	1876	-5	Myanmar	95	+6½
Japan	81	+9	Namibia	264	+1
Jordan	962	+2	Nauru	674	+12
Kazakhstan	7	+4/+6	Nepal	977	+5¾
Kenya	254	+3	Netherlands	31	+1
Kiribati	686	+12	Netherlands Antilles	599	-4
Kuwait	965	+3	New Caledonia	687	+11
Kyrgyzstan	996	+6	New Zealand	64	+12
Laos	856	+7	Nicaragua	505	-6
Latvia	371	+2	Niger	227	+1
Lebanon	961	+2	Nigeria	234	+1
Lesotho	266	+2	Niue	683	-11
Liberia	231	0	Norfolk Island	672	+11½
Libya	218	+1	Northern Marianas	1670	+10
Liechtenstein	423	+1	North Korea	850	+9

INTERNATIONAL INFORMATION

COUNTRY	DIALLING CODE	HOURS DIFF. FROM GMT	COUNTRY	DIALLING CODE	HOURS DIFF. FROM GMT
Norway	47	+1	Spain	34	+1
Oman	968	+4	Sri Lanka	94	+6
Pakistan	92	+5	Sudan	249	+2
Palau	680	+9	Suriname	597	-3
Panama	507	-5	Swaziland	268	+2
Papua New Guinea	675	+10	Sweden	46	+1
Paraguay	595	-4	Switzerland	41	+1
Peru	51	-5	Syria	963	+2
Philippines	63	+8	Taiwan	886	+8
Poland	48	+1	Tajikistan	992	+6
Portugal	351	0	Tanzania	255	+3
Puerto Rico	1787	-4	Thailand	66	+7
Qatar	974	+3	Togo	228	0
Réunion	262	+4	Tonga	676	+13
Romania	40	+2	Trinidad and Tobago	1868	-4
Russian Federation	7	+2/+11	Tunisia	216	+1
Rwanda	250	+2	Turkey	90	+2
St Helena	290	0	Turkmenistan	993	+5
St Kitts and Nevis	1869	-4	Turks and Caicos Islands	1649	-5
St Lucia	1758	-4	Tuvalu	688	+12
St Pierre and Miquelon	508	-3	Uganda	256	+3
St Vincent and the Grenadines	1784	-4	Ukraine	380	+2
Samoa	685	-11	United Arab Emirates	971	+4
San Marino	378	+1	United Kingdom	44	0
São Tomé and Principe	239	0	United States of America	1	-5/-10
Saudi Arabia	966	+3	Uruguay	598	-3
Senegal	221	0	Uzbekistan	998	+5
Serbia and Montenegro	381	+1	Vanuatu	678	+11
Seychelles	248	+4	Venezuela	58	-4
Sierra Leone	232	0	Vietnam	84	+7
Singapore	65	+8	Virgin Islands (UK)	1284	-4
Slovakia	421	+1	Virgin Islands (US)	1340	-4
Slovenia	386	+1	Wallis and Futuna	681	+12
Solomon Islands	677	+11	Yemen	967	+3
Somalia	252	+3	Yugoslavia	381	+1
South Africa	27	+2	Zambia	260	+2
South Korea	82	+9	Zimbabwe	263	+2

CENTIMETRES TO INCHES

cm		inches
2.54	1	0.39
5.08	2	0.79
7.62	3	1.81
10.1	4	1.57
12.7	5	1.97
15.2	6	2.36
17.8	7	2.76
20.3	8	3.15
22.9	9	3.54
25.4	10	3.94
27.9	11	4.33
30.4	12	4.72

METRES TO FEET

metres		feet
0.30	1	3.3
0.61	2	6.6
0.91	3	9.8
1.22	4	13.1
1.52	5	16.4
1.83	6	19.7
2.13	7	23.0
2.44	8	26.2
2.74	9	29.5
3.05	10	32.8

KILOGRAMS TO POUNDS

kg		lb
0.45	1	2.2
0.91	2	4.4
1.36	3	6.6
1.81	4	8.8
2.27	5	11.0
2.72	6	13.2
3.18	7	15.4
3.63	8	17.6
4.08	9	19.8
4.54	10	22.0

CELSIUS TO FAHRENHEIT

°c	°f
-10	14
-5	23
0	32
5	41
10	50
15	59
20	68
25	77
30	86
35	95
40	104
45	113
50	122

KILOMETRES TO MILES

km	miles
10	6.2
20	12.4
30	18.6
40	24.9
50	31.1
60	37.3
70	43.5
80	49.5
90	55.9
100	62.1

LITRES TO GALLONS

litres		gallons
4.5	1	0.22
9.1	2	0.44
13.6	3	0.66
18.2	4	0.88
22.7	5	1.10
27.3	6	1.32
31.8	7	1.54
36.4	8	1.76
40.9	9	1.98
45.5	10	2.20

WOMEN'S SUITS AND DRESSES

American	British	Continental
6	8	36
8	10	38
10	12	40
12	14	42
14	16	44
16	18	46
18	20	48

MEN'S SUITS AND OVERCOATS

American	British	Continental
36	36	46
38	38	48
40	40	50
42	42	52
44	44	54

MEN'S SHIRTS

American	British	Continental
14	14	36
14½	14½	37
15	15	38
15½	15½	39
16	16	41
16½	16½	42
17	17	43

MEN'S SHOES

American	British	Continental
8	7	40
9	8	41
10	9	42
11	10	43
12	11	44
13	12	45

WOMEN'S SHOES

American	British	Continental
6	4	38
7	5	39
8	6	40
9	7	41
10	8	42

USEFUL ADDRESSES

USEFUL ADDRESSES

Palmyra, Syria

USEFUL ADDRESSES

USEFUL ADDRESSES

Angkor, Cambodia

USEFUL ADDRESSES